# PORT and SHERRY

GEORGE SANDEMAN
of Perth, London and Oporto
founder of the Sandeman firm in 1790
born 1765 – died 1841

# PORT and SHERRY

## The story of two fine wines

GEO. G. SANDEMAN SONS & CO. LIMITED

LONDON

Made and printed in Great Britain by Lund Humphries & Co. Ltd.

# Preface

*This short book will, it is hoped, answer those questions which sometimes puzzle consumers of both Port and Sherry wines.*

*There are no doubt many who, through lack of the necessary information regarding decanting etc., may not always attain the fullest enjoyment of them.*

*The present work which is written in everyday terms, and avoids technicalities, is addressed especially to them, its main purpose being to help and interest lovers of fine wines in such ways as will enable them to buy wisely, store safely, handle, serve and enjoy both Port and Sherry to the best advantage.*

*With these objects in view, it traces the history of these wines, describes how they are made, gives clear details of their inherent peculiarities, and advises on their decanting, uses in cuisine etc., etc., together with a map which will be useful to readers who visit the Peninsula. There are, moreover, many photographic plates which should prove of interest.*

*Long practical experience is a prerequisite to the making, maturing and tending of Port and Sherry wines before they reach the public, to preserve their fine qualities and to ensure a high standard of uniformity in their various styles.*

*It is equally important to know just how to treat these wines in such a way as to be certain they maintain their original excellencies to the time when they are served, in order that they can be enjoyed to the full.*

*Wine is alive and its life must be protected against deleterious influences; these and the simple means of circumventing them are explained, together with many other aspects of importance a knowledge of which will increase your enjoyment of two of nature's richest gifts.*

*This volume, though slender, contains the experience of 165 years, compressed for your easy assimilation, and its perusal will doubtless add to your appreciation of both wines.*

*May I suggest that you read this little book leisurely, just as a good Port or Sherry should be drunk?*

LONDON 1955

Patrick W. Sandeman

# List of illustrations

# The historical background of Port wine

The story of Port wine should, we think, open with some historical references. That the trade in wine between Great Britain and Portugal is of ancient origin is evidenced by the fact that it can be traced back to the days of barter *Barter* between seafarers of the two countries.

It was in 1308 that the first Anglo-Portuguese Com- *1308 Treaty* mercial Treaty was concluded; and this was superseded by the Treaty of 1353 which among its provisions per- *1353 Treaty* mitted Portuguese fishermen to fish off the English coast. There is evidence that this led to the exchange of wine (which the Portuguese carried for their own consumption) for British goods. This wine was not, however, Port wine as we know it now (the character of which was developed later), but was an unfortified table wine which is still drunk throughout Portugal.

Thereafter successive Agreements culminated in the Treaty of Windsor which was signed in London on 9 May *Treaty of Windsor* 1386. This treaty envisaged a lasting alliance and reci- *1386* procal military aid between the two countries. From this time England enjoyed many trading facilities with Portugal, and was regarded by the Portuguese as a commercially favoured nation. By 1578 the export of Portuguese wine to England from Viana do Castelo, a small town on the coast some fifty miles north of Oporto, had become sufficiently important to warrant the appointment of a British consul there. It was not, however, until about 1670 that wines from the Douro region were exported in any appreciable quantity.

*Methuen Treaty 1703*

There is little doubt that the treaty negotiated by The Rt. Hon. John Methuen and signed on 27 December 1703 (which came to be known as the *Methuen Treaty*) had a most invigorating effect on the import of Portuguese wines into Britain in that it conceded lower duty charges than those imposed on French and German wines.

*The Oporto Wine Company*

In 1755 a Spanish merchant, one Don Bartoleme Pancorvo initiated The Oporto Wine Company. This virtual monopoly was, however, strongly opposed by British traders, and failed in the year of its foundation. But in the following year the powerful Marquis of Pombal revived and amended the scheme that had failed and it continued to function with varying vicissitudes (which included armed attack and incendiarism) until 1833.

Among the many regulations which he propounded was one which has had lasting beneficial effects. We refer to the geographical demarcation of what is now the

*The Douro District*

famous 'Douro District'. The underlying intention of this demarcation was to ear-mark that area of the Douro valley from which the finest wines emanate, thereby ensuring the quality of Port wine produced for export. That the original limits of the prescribed area were quickly decreased, it being found that they embraced terrain in which certain inferior table wines were grown, and the fact that many subsequent reductions have been made, does not detract one iota from the Marquis's admirable intention.

The present officially demarcated area of the Douro district extends from some sixty miles up river from

Oporto, and roughly between the village of Mezão Frio in the West, to Barca d'Alva on the Spanish frontier in the East, a total area of some 1250 square miles.

Despite this undoubted benefaction to present-day consumers of Port wine, The Oporto Wine Company was deprived of its powers in May 1834, and a period of commercial freedom ensued during which trade declined until 1838, when Queen Maria II reinstated it in a very modified form.

With the passage of time however, this company (in any form) became less and less acceptable to both British traders and Douro wine farmers, until it was expunged finally in 1858. It should however be recorded that, during its régime 'The Company' eliminated doubtful methods of production which had threatened, to which extent it served posterity well.

In December 1888 the idea of forming yet another Government sponsored and subsidized Monopoly Company was mooted, but it came to nothing.

ESTABLISHMENT OF THE HOUSE OF SANDEMAN

For historical facts of a more intimate nature, we revert now to the year 1790 in which George Sandeman, a member of an old Scottish family, first recorded in Alyth in 1594, founded the House of Sandeman in London.

That he was a man of ambition, determination and abounding confidence is shown by a letter which he wrote to his sister in May 1790. Therein he declared that he would not return to Perth (of which city he became a freeman) until he had made a moderate fortune with which to retire, and to accomplish that end he allowed himself nine years unless, as he said: 'some fortunate circumstance should reduce the time to five or six years.'

Abundantly optimistic as he was, he can hardly have imagined that the business of his modest wine vault, to assist him in the purchase of which his father had lent him £300, would grow to world-wide proportions, with vast Port wine lodges in Oporto, and extensive Sherry bodegas at Jerez.

*£300 loan*

Until 1796 George Sandeman had his brother David with him, but by 1798 the partnership had been amicably dissolved, and David Sandeman devoted his energies to founding the Commercial Bank of Scotland.

The establishment of George Sandeman's business came at a most opportune time. Troubles in France, in 1788, had fostered the importation of Portuguese wines to replace those from France which had been favoured in Britain previously. And this trend was furthered by the preferential treatment accorded by the Methuen Treaty, to which we have referred.

It was fortunate for him also, that towards the end of the eighteenth century, the conditions essential to the production of fine Port wine had been discovered; and by 1790 this knowledge had been applied to Douro wines to the extent that they became firm favourites with the English.

It was auspicious also that the origin of the House of Sandeman coincided with the appearance of true Vintage Port as we know it; and George Sandeman shipped the 1790 vintage, which was exemplary of Port wine at its best.

*Vintage 1790*

George Sandeman transacted his business for a short time at 'Tom's' coffee-house in Birchin Lane, Cornhill, in the City of London. This may seem strange by modern standards, but it was customary during the eighteenth

*Tom's coffee-house*

No.13 Sherborne Lane, George Sandeman's City residence as it appeared in 1805.

century for city merchants and businessmen to do considerable business in London's many coffee-houses; and it was in fact in 'Lloyd's' coffee-house that the now world-famous Insurance Institution of that name was born in 1770.

George Sandeman rented his own offices later at 24 *First offices*

5

Beating the Bounds in Sandeman's Vaults at 20 St. Swithins Lane.

Old Jewry; and despite The Peninsular War and other continental turmoils, he travelled considerably in both Portugal and Spain where the future of his business lay. While thus engaged he made many friends in the British Army amongst which he numbered the Duke of Wellington of whom he was a frequent guest.

*St. Swithins Lane and Sherborne Lane*   By 1805 he was able to secure the lease of 20 St. Swithins Lane as offices and wine vaults, together with the adjoining premises 13 Sherborne Lane, as a residence for himself and his family. These premises which back one

6

upon the other, are still the headquarters of the Company.

It is interesting in passing to note that the original inventory (13 April 1805) of fittings and fixtures which he took over at St. Swithins Lane, included:—

A Capital Patent Crane with three iron wheels, Jib Roller, Rope, Pulleys and Jigger.

*Capital Patent Crane*

This mechanism, which is not less than 135 years old and may be much older, is still in position and when the modern hydraulic lift which is now used was seriously damaged by enemy action in 1940, this 'Capital Crane' was invaluable (after being equipped with a new rope) in removing stocks of old vintage wines from the St. Swithins Lane Vaults to safer surroundings.

In these vaults beneath the firm's headquarters the boundaries of two London Parishes (St. Swithun and St. Mary Abchurch) meet, and are marked by two metal plaques dated 1784 and 1850.

Up to the outbreak of the Second World War it was the custom of the Parish Clergy, Beadles and Choristers to visit the Sandeman vaults on a day adjacent to Rogation Sunday (three days before Ascension Day) to 'Beat the Bounds' with long willow sticks. And on these occasions the progress of the Bounds-beating procession was, as might be expected, apt to be delayed while its adult members emulated the ancient performers of this undoubtedly pre-Christian rite: for is it not a remnant of the Festival of Terminalia which was dedicated to the God Terminus, guardian of fields and landmarks, at which the Romans celebrated with rich Falernian and other wines?

*Beating the Bounds*

It is a matter of some interest in this connection to note that, while latterly the ceremony consisted mainly in the younger element beating the ground where the two

7

Parishes meet, it was they who in earlier times were soundly thrashed at the boundary marks, to ensure that they remembered the location of their Parish boundaries.

George Sandeman who was the last man to go on 'Change' in breeches and top boots, and wore also a white *'Old Cauliflower'* wig from which he was nicknamed 'Old Cauliflower', died in Brussels in 1841; and was succeeded by his nephew George Glas Sandeman (1792–1868), who widened the scope of the business in several directions.

These included insurance and the export of linen and Manchester cotton goods to the West Indies, Central America and Mexico. The new undertakings were not, however, to the detriment of his wine business, which continued to flourish to the extent that the Firm then ran its own clipper the *Hoopoe* between Oporto and the east coast ports of England.

This 86-ton ship, built in 1865, remained in the Company's service till *circa* 1875, when she was sold.

It would appear that her Master, one R. Crathorn, took delight in making rapid passages to such an extent that the cost of repairing her sheets made her uneconomical as a means of transport. The *Hoopoe* was subsequently posted missing outward bound from Prawle in Devon, on 3 October 1878.

Albert George Sandeman (1833–1923) his eldest son, succeeded George Glas Sandeman in 1868 and took his three brothers into partnership. One of them, Colonel John Glas Sandeman, had the honour as a subaltern of the 1st Royal Dragoons, of taking part in the Charge of the Heavy Brigade at Balaclava. It is interesting to record also, that it was he who with the aid of a mechanic, one *Penny-in-the-slot* Everett, invented the-penny-in-the-slot machine, which *machine*

Extract from George Sandeman's original letter dated London 1790, in which he solicits a loan of £300.

The Sandeman clipper *Hoopoe*, built in 1865, and posted missing in October 1878.

The world-famous Sandeman Don figure trade-mark.

was patented in their combined names. Albert George Sandeman strengthened the family connection with the Peninsula, when in 1856 he married the eldest daughter of the Visconde da Torre de Moncorvo, then Ambassador at the Court of St. James.

A man of considerable business acumen and drive, he was a Director of the Bank of England and was created its Governor in 1896 and 1897.

The Partnership which he had formed was converted into a Private Limited Company in 1902, and it was as head of this Company that his eldest son Walter Albert Sandeman (1858–1937) succeeded him in 1923. Under his Chairmanship this old-fashioned family business was brought into line with modern commercial practice. And by harnessing the benefits of advertising to good products, he secured a world-wide goodwill for the name of Sandeman. Towards this end, the acquisition in 1928 of the Company's now universally known Don figure trade-mark, and its continuous use in conjunction with the name SANDEMAN in distinctive block capital letters (which had been registered previously as a trade-mark) were, and continue to be, of considerable value as recognition data for both the House of Sandeman and its wines. That W. A. Sandeman was jealous of the very name Port, and zealous in the interests of both the Port Wine Trade in general and consumers of this wine (which is so ideally suited to the climate and taste of the British) in particular, was made clear in the first year of his control, through an action which he instituted in the Courts.

This case, a prosecution under the Merchandise Marks Act 1887, and the Anglo-Portuguese Commercial Treaty Acts 1914 and 1916, was heard summarily before Justices

*Private Limited Company*

*The Don figure trade-mark and the registered name*

11

of the Peace, sitting in Petty Sessions at Mortlake, Surrey, who, after hearing the evidence, dismissed the information, which was to the effect that a trader had, contrary to the Merchandise Marks Act, sold a bottle of wine, bearing a false trade description, namely, 'Tarragona Port'.

The Justices were thereupon asked by the Prosecution (Geo. G. Sandeman Sons & Co., Limited) to state a case for the opinion of the High Court of Justice, where on the matter being heard the following judgments were delivered (extract):–

### LORD CHIEF JUSTICE HEWART

The material fact is, that upon the 9th January of this year (1923) the Respondent did sell to a certain person a quart bottle of red Spanish wine known as 'Tarragona', bearing a label on which were printed the words 'Tarragona Port'. Even before the year 1914 it might have been difficult to justify such a sale . . .

The first section of the Anglo-Portuguese Commercial Treaty Act 1914 provides, so far as the word 'Port' is concerned:–

'That the description "port" applied to *any wine or other liquor* other than wine the produce of Portugal shall be deemed to be a false trade description within the meaning of the Merchandise Marks Act 1887 and that Act shall have effect accordingly.'

### Continuing his Lordship said:–

In my opinion, the provisions of that section made *impossible* the kind of argument and defence which were put forward on behalf of the Respondent in this case. . . . the subsequent Anglo-Portuguese Commercial Treaty Act of 1916, which became law on the 23rd August 1916 . . . adds to the earlier Act, and does not subtract from it . . .

### Therein it is made clear that:–

. . . it is not enough that the wine should come from Portugal, but there must be also a certificate issued by the competent Portuguese authorities to the effect that it was a wine to which by the law of Portugal the description 'port' may be applied.

*In my opinion, after the passing of the Act of 1914, this case was unarguable, and the appeal ought to be allowed, and the Justices should be directed to convict.*

Mr Justice Sankey and Mr Justice Salter sitting with the Lord Chief Justice agreed.

On his death in 1937 Walter Albert Sandeman was succeeded by his son Henry Gerard Walter Sandeman (1885–1953).

A personality of great charm, shrewd and meticulous, he maintained and enhanced the Company's interests and the family business traditions with assiduity. He succumbed to serious illness in 1952; and just before his death in January 1953, he was succeeded by his brother Patrick Walter Sandeman the Company's present Chairman, who has the support of his two sons, Timothy Walter Sandeman and David Patrick Sandeman, on the Company's Board.

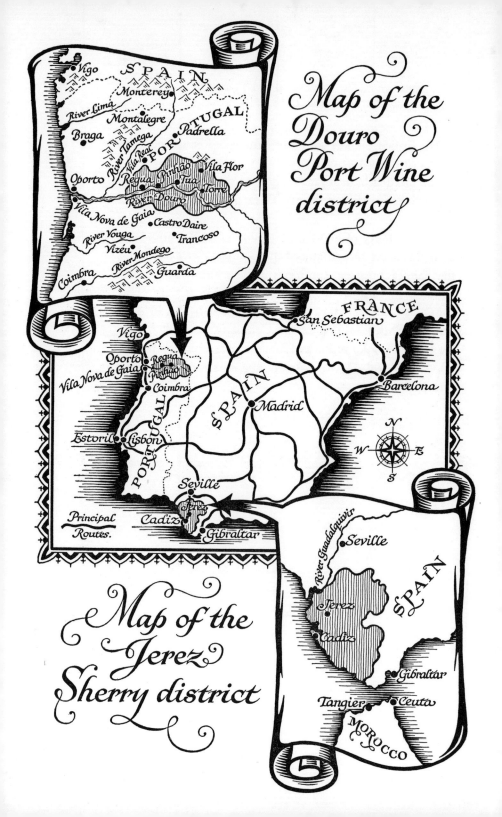

Map of the Douro Port Wine district

Map of the Jerez Sherry district

# PORT
# from Portugal

That the unique characteristics of Port wine are safe-guarded in Great Britain (and some other countries) by both Act and Treaty, we have seen from the preceding brief historical outline.

## SOIL AND CLIMATE

The distinctive qualities of Port wine are not so much attributable to the method of its production as to the geological and climatic conditions in which the vines are grown. Throughout the precipitous delineated Douro region, to which we have alluded, the soil is impregnated with a soft foliated stone known as schist, and it is from *Schist* this that much of the wine's uniqueness is derived.

The country in which this geological condition prevails, being precipitous, the hillsides are cut into walled terraces to ensure that the torrential rains which often occur in this area do not uproot the vines that are planted on these great steps in rows from 2½ to 4 feet apart. Visitors to the Douro district can hardly fail to remark on the herculean task of building up these terraces on the hillsides, which it has taken centuries to accomplish.

As to the climate of the Douro district, shade tempera- *Temperature* tures can exceed 100°F in the summer, and the winter is sometimes extremely cold, when deep snow is no rarity.

The productivity of the schistose soil of the area varies *Productivity*

15

according to its schist content. In the lower Douro 1000 vines may give from two to six pipes (115 gallons each) of wine. But on the more rugged slopes of the 'Upper Douro' where the ground is mainly schist with little soil, the yield is barely one pipe of wine per thousand vines. Wines from this area are, however, of superior quality.

Taken as a whole the Douro district is capable of producing over 160,000 pipes of Port wine *per annum*. The *Governmental limit* Portuguese Government however sets a limit each year to the amount of wine to be produced as Port; and the surplus is either made into unfortified table wine for local consumption, or is distilled to produce Brandy.

Before considering the matter of the production of Port wine, allusion should we think be made to the great *Phylloxera scourge* *Phylloxera* scourge, which by 1880 had wrought havoc in the Douro vineyards. The cause of this disaster was the so-called plant louse of America, a creature so small that it can hardly be seen with the naked eye, which breeds prolifically, and with incredible speed.

These small insects which live on the thin roots of the vine, sapping the vitality of the plant to the point of death, decimated whole tracts of the Douro vineyards. Their depredations were however subsequently overcome by replanting the district with American vines which were immune from the disease, and grafting Portuguese vines on to them. Some of the best known varieties were *Mourisco*, *Tinta Francisca* and *Touriga*, the grapes of which display practically all the special characteristics of the original indigenous vines and yield much juice and sugar.

PRODUCTION

How then is this wine which is so ideally suited to

our climate produced? Let us examine the happenings.

Towards the end of September, when the vintage usually begins, bands of vintagers, many from far distant villages, trek to the vineyards equipped with small hooked knives with which they detach the bunches of grapes. *The vintage*

Having severed the grapes, any immature or unsound fruit is removed and the sound fruit is placed in baskets that the vintagers carry with them. These vintagers' baskets are emptied later into larger ones, holding upwards of a hundredweight of fruit, to be carried to the press-houses by men moving in single file. Here the grapes are placed in *lagars* (stone tanks), which hold sufficient fruit for the production after pressing, of ten to twenty pipes of wine. *Press-houses and lagars*

The grapes are then trodden, a process which, with periods of rest, sometimes continues for several days to the accompaniment of music and high-spirited banter. While this procedure may appear to be antiquated, it is superior to any other, in that the richness and colour of the 'must' (freshly pressed juice of grapes) are retained, without the pips of the fruit being crushed, thus avoiding excess astringency. *Treading*

After the grapes have been pressed, the 'must' is left in the *lagars* to ferment. Fermentation turns the sugar content of the wine into alcohol; and it will be seen from this, that the longer fermentation is allowed to continue the more 'dry' (less sweet) the wine becomes. To ensure that the desired degree of sweetness is retained, a saccharometer (instrument for measuring sweetness) is used. Then to curtail fermentation at the appropriate point, the 'must' is drawn off the *lagar* into large vats or tonnels and *Fermentation* mixed with a quantity of pure grape Brandy. This arrests the fermentation immediately and has the combined effect of producing Port wine which retains the requisite natural sweetness and has the desired alcoholic strength.

*New wine*    These new wines remain in the vats till the end of the year. Later they are drawn off into pipes which have been sent from Oporto in readiness; and in the spring their journey begins from the *Quintas* (wine growing farms) of the Alto Douro to the 'lodges' or overground wine stores in Vila Nova de Gaia, a town on the opposite bank of the

*The name Port*    Douro river from Oporto, from which latter town Port wine takes its name.

We should interpolate here that the casks of various sizes (pipes, hogsheads and quartercasks) used by Sandemans, are all made in their own extensive cooperage; and their construction in oak calls for craftsmanship of a very high order, the art of which is passed from father to son from generation to generation.

*Transport*    Ox-carts are still used to carry the pipes through the narrow and tortuous tracks from many of the outlying wine farmsteads, and through the restricted by-ways of the vineyards which lie in the valleys and at the river's edge. Thereafter they are transported down the Douro river to Oporto in traditional craft, the long trailing rudders of which are wielded with consummate skill, to pilot the precious cargo through the rapids and between rocks that in parts of the river are dangerous. In these days, however, more and more wine is being transported by road and railway.

*Oporto*    Viewed from the river the city of Oporto presents an interesting vista of quaint architecture, and on the opposite bank in Vila Nova de Gaia the spacious lodges of the

Typical Douro vineyards.

Gathering grapes in a sun-drenched Douro vineyard.

Moving in single file, men carry grapes to the press-houses
*(from an old water-colour drawing)*.

The waterfront at Oporto *(the Sandeman lodges are outlined)*.

Ox-carts are still used in Vila Nova de Gaia.

General view of the Vila Nova quay, showing shipments of Sandeman Port ready for loading *(Oporto in the distance)*.

The interior of a Sandeman Lodge.

House of Sandeman await this new wine, which, in due course, will be used either for blending with, or refreshing, existing stocks of more mature wine.

When the vintage is exceptionally good, some of the *Vintage Port* new wine is segregated in case it develops sufficiently to be shipped as 'Vintage Port'.

Literally thousands of pipes of wine in varying stages of maturity lie in the lodges three tiers high over the length and breadth of the vast floor space, where they receive the constant care of experts of long experience, who regularly refresh them and subsequently blend them suitably for export to all parts of the world.

When very young, the so-called 'Red Ports' are of a *Red Port* rich purple colour and are termed 'full' wines. It is however in the nature of Port wine to lose colour with age and development; and in time it becomes progressively Ruby, Light Ruby, Medium Tawny and Tawny in colour, its original purple hue having disappeared during the first few years.

These wines, which are matured in casks, are of the type which is purchased as standard Port wine, and are known in the trade as 'Port from the Wood', to distinguish *Port from the Wood* them from 'Vintage Port', *with which they must not be confused*.

Port from the Wood is a blend of wines of different years, so married as to combine the best qualities of each and to produce a balanced wine of consistent quality which does not vary, and upon which you can therefore rely. Thus, if you purchase Port wine by name, as supplied by a reputable shipper, you are assured of the constancy of both its quality and style.

There are, thanks to skilled blenders, various styles of *Various styles*

23

Sandeman Port, one or other of which will suit all palates and needs. In some countries the richer and more full-bodied wines are preferred. In others wines of lighter, drier finish, are in greater demand; and it is to meet these varying tastes that large stocks of wine from different years, together with skill in tending and blending them, are so essential. The blending is carried out in huge vats some of which have a capacity of up to 100 pipes. The *White Port* production of White Port is carried out in precisely the same way, the only difference being that white grapes are used.

VINTAGE PORT

Having warned our reader against confusing Port from the Wood with 'Vintage' Ports, some explanation is required. While Ports from the Wood are matured in cask and blended from wines of different years, 'Vintage' Ports are selected portions of the wine of a superlatively good year, and are not blended with the wine of any other year.

In order to retain its body and supreme characteristics 'Vintage' Port is matured in casks in Oporto *for two years only*, after which it is shipped to England or elsewhere and is bottled immediately. From this point the wine continues to mature in the bottle, on the lower inside of which it throws a thick 'crust', meanwhile acquiring what is known as 'bottle age' or 'bottle flavour'.

While it is usual to ship and bottle 'Vintage' Ports two or three years after the vintage, and most shippers favour the shorter period, there are small quantities of what are *Late-bottled-* known as 'Late-bottled-Vintage-Ports'. These exceptional *Vintage-Ports* wines are kept three, four or even five years in cask before they are bottled, during which time they deposit much of their body in the form of 'lees' (precipitate) and lose colour in the cask. They are thus lighter in every way than wines which are bottled earlier and do not exhibit the characteristics of a true 'Vintage' Port to the same degree as those which are bottled two years after the vintage.

This being so, practically all the leading shippers agreed some years ago not to offer any Port as 'Vintage' wine (the wine of a single year) if it had been kept in cask for more than seven years. The reason for this being, that it is necessary to refresh all Ports which have been kept in cask for any length of time with younger wines.

A true 'Vintage' Port which retains its magnificent colour and body always throws a thick 'crust' in course of time. Continuity of cellarage is therefore most important *Cellarage* because, after the crust has formed, the bottles should not be moved more than is absolutely necessary until the wine is decanted for use, regarding which delicate process some comment will, we hope, be helpful.

Years ago it was customary to mark all wines which, like 'Vintage' Port throw a 'crust' or deposit, with a splash of whitewash to indicate the upper surface of the bottle as it lay in the bin, which in turn indicated the position of the 'crust', *i.e.* immediately below the white-wash, on the inner undersurface of the bottle. Sandemans use a label for this purpose believing that it serves the additional purpose of identifying the contents of the bottle at a glance.

When about to decant a crusted wine, remove it very *Decanting* carefully from the bin, label uppermost, and place it gently into a wicker cradle or still better, stand the bottle upright some hours before it is required. Then holding the bottle firmly, remove the sealing-wax from the end of the cork (which may have become soft) and extract it.

The best type of cork-screw for the purpose is one with a plain wire spiral (no cutting edge) which is less liable to pull through the cork without extracting it. Having removed the cork successfully, the wine can be decanted off the 'crust' with practically no loss. If however the 'crust' should slip or become disturbed, it is advisable either to have a fine strainer or a funnel and three or four folds of clean muslin handy with which to strain the wine. It is nevertheless preferable to avoid straining if at all possible. As is the case in so many instances, practice makes perfect when decanting fine wine.

*Boot and Flogger*

In this connection it is interesting to note that Sandemans still cork their vintage Ports by the old 'Boot and Flogger' method. This, though quaint and somewhat slow, has a worthwhile advantage.

The operator sits with a cylindrical leather cup (known as the 'boot') strapped to his left knee, into which he places the bottle to be corked. He then takes a cork moistened in wine and beats it into the bottle neck with a wooden lath or 'flogger'.

When a mechanical cork-driver is used it thrusts the cork into the bottle so far that the end of the cork is below the rim of the bottle neck. This offers poor anchorage for the sealing wax, which is applied as a closure to these fine wines. But when a cork is flogged into a bottle, it is not possible to drive it in even level with the lip of the bottle neck, and the head of the cork is therefore turned over by the beating into a shallow mushroom shape, the undercut of which provides an excellent grip for the wax, thus ensuring a perfect seal.

There is quite a lot of confusion regarding the length *Time in bottle*
of time that either a full-bodied 'Port from the Wood' or a
'Vintage' wine should be kept in bottle. This must, of
course, depend both on the wine itself and on individual
taste. It will, however, be quite obvious that a very
full-bodied deep-coloured wine is not calculated to arrive at
its state of perfection so quickly as a lighter or riper wine.
It is generally recognized that the vintages of more recent
years do not tend to be so full bodied as those of bygone
days. They should therefore reach maturity after seven
to ten years in bottle, they will, however, continue to
develop and improve for many years thereafter.

Richard Barham's dictum in the *Ingoldsby Legends* puts
this matter in perspective. He writes:–

> Though Port should have age
> Yet I don't think it sage
> To entomb it as some of your *connoisseurs* do
> Till it's losing in flavour and body and hue
> I question if keeping it does it much good
> After ten years in bottle and three in the wood

The immortal Jorrocks also betrayed little admiration for
excessively old Port when he said:–

But mind, I doesn't call the oldest the best – far from it – it's often
times the wust – No! Give me a good fruity wine – a wine with a grip
o' the Gob that leaves a mark on the side of the glass.

Both Barham and Surtees were authorities!

Sandemans hold what is probably the largest stock of
'Vintage' Ports in the world today, and have seldom, if
ever, been at fault in their selection of a 'Vintage' year.
For the past 165 years they have shipped the pick of Port
wine vintages only. These include the 1847's, 63's, 78's,
81's, 84's, 87's, 90's etc., none of which are available today.

The truth is, that the really old 'Vintage' Ports shipped by Sandeman were consumed long ago by a discerning public. The more recent Sandeman Vintages include the 1927's, 34's and 35's.

The 1935 vintage grown in the Jubilee year of King George V was bottled in black 'granite shotted' bottles in the Coronation year of King George VI. And to commemorate these historic occasions, the opposite shoulders of the bottles bore medallions suitably inscribed.

*Granite shotting*

The process of 'granite shotting', whereby the interior of the bottle is roughened or scored by granite chips, is undertaken to provide a grip for the 'crust' of the wine, thus rendering decanting without disturbing it less difficult.

With the advent of the Second World War the shipping of 'Vintage' Ports was prevented; and it was not until later that it was possible to ship small quantities of 1942's, 43's, 45's and 47's, all of which had been bottled in Oporto.

The 1950 vintage was bottled in Bond in England, and the coming of the next vintage is, at the time of writing (1954) an enigma, the solution of which only time can give.

*Selecting Port*

The selection of Port wine depends mainly upon whether it is required for 'laying down' and keeping for consumption at a much later date, or for immediate use. For 'laying down' either a young 'Vintage' or a full-bodied Port from the Wood is ideal. Both of these wines will acquire a distinct 'bottle flavour' in a few years, which enhances their value considerably.

For immediate consumption, freshly bottled Ports from the Wood which range in style from full-bodied fruity wines to the most delicate Light Tawnies and White Ports are the obvious choice.

Be your selection what it may, Sandemans have a Port wine which will meet your requirement admirably. From the grape to the glass, from the vineyards to your table, every detail from the pressing of the fruit to the bottling of your wine is under their supervision. From the time of their establishment in 1790 to the present day, there has been a continuity of family control which has preserved that knowledge and judgment which are so essential in the production and tending of fine wines. These qualities are indeed a heritage from generations past which have been passed from father to son with scrupulous attention to the finer details, on the principle that 'Trifles make Perfection but Perfection is no Trifle'. *Close supervision*

That this thorough first-hand training has been eminently successful is amply demonstrated by the highest awards for the quality of Sandeman wines gained at Exhibitions and Wine Congresses throughout the world. *Highest awards*

Sandemans have also been honoured by Special Appointment as Purveyors of Wine to the Royal Households of Great Britain, Denmark and Sweden, the late Royal Households of Spain, Portugal and Russia; and they have furnished wines for the Papal State of the Vatican. They believe with Ruskin and avoid the tendency to which he refers when he wrote:–

There is hardly anything in the world that some men cannot make a little worse and sell a little cheaper, and the people who consider prices only are those men's legitimate prey. The sweetness of low prices is lost by the bitterness of poor quality.

It has therefore come about that the name Sandeman is synonymous with choice Port and Sherry the world over.

Let us now turn to some of those details which, though they have not as yet been mentioned in this short monograph, will we hope be of interest to appreciators of that wine of which Tennyson wrote:–

> Oh plump head-waiter at the 'Cock'
> To which I most resort!
> How goes the time? 'Tis five o'clock
> Go fetch a pint of Port:
> But let it not be such as that
> You set before chance-comers
> But such whose father-grape grows fat
> On Lusitanian Summers.

Where to begin our discussion of these details presents a problem in that they are not a few, and have many and varied implications.

First perhaps a timely reminder should be given that *Store Port lying flat* your Port wine must be kept lying flat before it is opened; with the wine against the cork and the label uppermost. This will enable you to know the whereabouts of any 'crust' or deposit that may form while the wine is recumbent, and will facilitate decanting the wine off the deposit, when this is necessary.

If several bottles of Port are stored together in this way, make sure that they are securely placed to avoid the others slipping or rolling when a bottle is removed.

*Bins* Wood or metal bins (racks) of sizes suitable for fitting into convenient cupboards are perfect for this purpose, as each bottle lies in its own section of the bin.

*Temperature of* The temperature of your wine store should be even, *store* from 60°F to 62°F is ideal, because it is in the nature of all wines to 'throw' a deposit, and either too low or fluctuating temperatures will hasten or retard this process.

Even when the wine is kept in an equable temperature

An expert flogs a cork home.

A 'Tulip' glass (*left*) and a 'Dock' glass, they both have artistic and practical merit.

it will in due course throw a deposit which, if allowed to permeate the wine through careless handling of the bottle, will destroy its brightness and mar its appearance. Care must therefore be taken to avoid this, and if the deposit is for any reason seriously disturbed, the wine must be decanted through three of four folds of muslin before it is served.

## AU CHAMBRÉ OR CHILLED

Port wine may be served either *au chambré* (at room temperature) as a dessert wine or slightly chilled as an aperitif. To ensure the former condition it should be left two or three hours in the room in which it is to be used, but must not be artificially warmed. Chilling for use as an aperitif is effected by a short sojourn in the refrigerator.

To serve Port wine chilled may appear to be heterodox as indeed was the use of tobacco, in the view of our fore-fathers, when drinking Port. This myth has however been exploded and there are few, who in these days would deny, that to smoke either a cigar or cigarette with a glass of Port is to enhance the pleasure of both. *Chilled Port*

*Smoking*

Apart from the fact that red wines and fish are anti-pathetic to one another, there are really no hard-and-fast rules as regards the wines that should be served with any particular course or dish. But, as we have premised, Port may be served either before or after a meal with every satisfaction. It is also a much appreciated occasional wine, and Port is of course the traditional wine in which Loyal and other toasts are honoured. *Serving occasions*

It is noteworthy that in the Royal Navy the Loyal Toast is honoured seated, both afloat and in shore messes, unless there is a band present.

## Port

This custom appears to have originated on an occasion when King George III made uncomfortable contact with the deck beam on rising to a toast during a visit to one of his ships. As a result, he ordained that thereafter officers of the Royal Navy should drink his health seated.

This would seem to be a likely explanation, as in old ships there was very little head room, and during rough weather chairs on board ship were fixed to the deck and could not be moved to facilitate rising.

As a finish to your dinner party, large or small, Sandeman Port served with creamy Stilton cheese, will make it a memorable occasion.

### GLASSES FOR PORT

In what glasses should Port be served? While the actual type and design of glass to be used with Port wine must to a great extent remain a matter of personal taste, two points in this connection are certain. Glasses for Port should be of generous dimension, but they should only be two-thirds filled. An over-filled glass neither makes for comfort nor does it permit of a proper appreciation of the bouquet of fine wine.

There is little room for doubt that Port looks at its best in a deep-cut-glass; but not a few experts hold, that fine wines taste better from the thinnest of plain white glasses. *Barrel or tulip glasses* A barrel or tulip-shaped glass which tapers gently towards its rim is perhaps the best type for most wines. In a glass of this pleasant and easy-to-handle shape, the bouquet of the wine is retained and can be enjoyed. It is for this very reason that wine-tasters and experts, whose noses tell them so much about a wine before they taste it, use what are *'Dock' glasses* known as 'Dock' glasses, which are in fact an elongated

34

tapering exaggeration of the shape which we have suggested for general use.

Having written of glasses for and the decanting of Port *Decanters* wine, some consideration of decanters is warranted. It is difficult to improve upon an eighteenth-century deep-cut-glass decanter for the display of a fine ruby wine. The perfectly balanced Georgian or 'Ship's' decanters with their broad bases are ideal; and to protect the surface of a mahogany table, an antique decanter stand or 'coaster' *Coasters* is both practical and ornamental.

A silver decanter-label is also a pleasant embellishment, *Silver labels* but it is perhaps most useful on occasions when a very large bottle (say a magnum) of some fine old wine is served from the original bottle, after having been decanted. Well polished and decorated with a silver chain and neck label, these bottles make a wonderful centrepiece for a table.

A 'magnum', by the way, is a bottle the capacity of *Bottle sizes* which is equal to that of two ordinary bottles which hold $26\frac{2}{3}$ fluid ounces. And it is perhaps appropriate here to mention the 'Tappit-Hen' that holds three normal bottles, the 'Jeroboam' with a capacity of four, and the noble 'Rehoboam' which contains six bottles of wine.

It is well nigh impossible to write of decanters without thinking of passing the Port, and let us say at once that in *Passing the Port* these islands the decanter is passed clockwise, *i.e.* from the right to left, and there appears to be a common-sense reason for this. The majority of people are right handed. If, therefore, the decanter or bottle is passed to them from the left, they are able to replenish their glass with their most accustomed hand, which under certain circumstances presages an element of added safety if nothing more. This custom is so firmly established that it might almost be regarded as a cult.

It is well to remember also, that some degree of unpopularity may accrue to any member of a party who either through forgetfulness or because they do not require any more wine, fails to 'top-up' their glass and pass the decanter on. Such people are sometimes referred *'Bottle-stoppers'* to as 'bottle-stoppers'. There is, of course, no question of etiquette involved by passing the decanter without refreshing one's glass, but it is usual to take a small token quantity when the wine reaches you.

This reminds us of the now defunct but nevertheless *Buzzing the* very interesting custom of 'Buzzing' the decanter or bottle, *decanter* which entailed a kind of wager. If when the decanter came to a member of the party he thought that it contained the precise amount of wine which would just fill his glass, without spilling a drop, and that by so doing he would completely empty the decanter or bottle, he declared a 'Buzz'. And if the 'Buzzer' was successful, the other members of the party were each required to 'stand' him a bottle, and *vice versa*. This procedure would seem to indicate that in the days gone by capacities for enjoying Port were greater than most moderns would care to admit.

### OTHER WAYS AND MEANS

It is neither our wish nor is it our intention to weary the reader with a monotonous recital of recipes. We should, however, be failing in our duty if we did not include some mention of other uses for Port wine than those to which we have referred. Pursuing the versatility of this great wine still further, we find that it is a valuable asset in many other directions.

There are several sauces which by the correct addition of Port are enhanced to a state of perfection that can only be assessed by trial. There is for example Cherry Sauce which is ideal with roast mutton, hare, venison, etc.

To prepare this, place a pound pot of black currant jelly into a stewpan with six ounces of preserved cherries, and a small stick of cinnamon and a dozen cloves tied in a muslin bag. Then add two generous glasses of Sandeman Ruby Port and simmer the whole for ten minutes. Now remove the spice bag and the sauce is ready to be served.

There is also the very economical Cumberland Sauce that will keep for a considerable time in a covered jar, which is excellent with many meat dishes served either hot or cold. All you need to prepare it is a pound of red currant jelly, to which add the juice of quarter of a lemon, one dessert-spoonful of Worcester Sauce, and a large glass of Sandeman Ruby Port. To these ingredients add the juice of half an orange, a handful of not too finely chopped preserved cherries and the peel of an orange cut into fine strips, you then have a memorable condiment.

A large glass of Ruby Port added when jugging hare improves this dish almost beyond belief. And as an addition to Christmas puddings and mincemeat, Port wine is distinguished.

In the summertime add a little Ruby Port to your fresh strawberries and cream. It will heighten the flavour of the fruit and help to neutralize its natural acidity.

Fraises Romanoff is yet another mouth-watering deli- cacy which is easily prepared.

Steep a pound of fresh ripe strawberries for an hour in a glass bowl with two glasses of Sandeman Ruby Port. Then immediately before serving add two or more large spoonsful of vanilla ice cream and an equal quantity of thick whipped cream. Stir them together gently without breaking the fruit, and you have a sweet *par excellence*.

*Cantaloup au Porto*  Have you tasted Cantaloup au Porto? It offers no difficulty in preparation. Just cut a small circular section from the top of a large ripe cantaloup melon and remove all the seeds with a long-handled spoon. Then pour a quarter of a bottle of Sandeman Ruby Port into the melon, add caster sugar and replace the cut portion. Now place the melon in the refrigerator and turn it occasionally so that all parts are well soaked with wine. Cut in the usual manner and served very cold, this is exquisite.

*Stewed prunes*  Even the humble stewed prune can be transformed out of all recognition by the addition of Sandeman Ruby Port and some thick cream.

Scores of other palate-tickling recipes in which Port wine plays a leading role are available for the benefit of those who will take the little trouble which is necessary to enhance many otherwise humdrum dishes to a point of excellence. They are all worthy of your second thoughts.

Armed with this outline of the growth and production of Port, we hope that our reader will feel at home with and have a greater appreciation of this unique wine.

# SHERRY
# from Spain

As was the case when we discussed Port wine, some historical allusions will, we believe, be of interest to the reader here.

The Andalusian town Jerez-de-la-Frontera, which was founded by the Phoenicians *circa* 1100 B.C. and called by them Shera, came later under the domination of the Greeks who perpetuated this name. Then in 206 B.C., the Romans renamed it Cerit or Ceritium; and it would seem from the writings of Columella, a citizen of Gades (Cadiz), who was an agricultural scribe in the first century A.D., and from archæological findings, that even at this early date Jerez (pronounced Herreth) was an important wine-growing centre.

It is interesting *en passant* to recollect that when the Barbarians invaded Spain in 409 A.D., the Vandals (one of their tribes) occupied an area which came to be known as Vandalusia (now Andalusia).

Following in the succession of invaders came the Moors and it was during their régime that the town's name became Xerez, which the Arabs pronounced Scheris. There would therefore appear to be little room for doubt that we have here the derivation of the English name given to wines from the Jerez district, *i.e.* Sherris in its earlier form, which later became Sherry (1608); and as such is a true geographical appellation. For as we shall see

later, it cannot be too rigorously stressed that the funda-
mental characteristics of Sherry wine are directly attributable to the nature of the soil and the climate which
prevails in the Jerez district.

While we are still discussing the name and geographical
implications of this most versatile of wines, it is amusing
to reflect that its name originated from the Moors who
were, by religious decree, total abstainers.

The history of Sherry may well have begun when in
*Alfonso the Wise* 1264 Alfonso X (called the Wise) lead his army into Jerez
and established a frontier between the Christians and the
Moslems.

For a hundred years thereafter Jerez was a focal point of
*Juan I* battle and in recognition of this Juan I accorded the
town the style Jerez-de-la-Frontera, in 1380. It was
however Alfonso the Wise who first encouraged the
making of wine and the extension of the vineyards round
Jerez, and from this the export of Spanish wines had its
small beginnings.

*Mediæval* That some Spanish wine came to this country in
*Spanish wine* mediæval days is certain. This wine was however sweet
in the main, and had neither the character nor the wide
range of Sherry as we know it today. It would not be
unreasonable to suppose that the universal sweetness of
the very early Spanish wines was directly attributable to
the Moorish prohibition régime, during which only un-
fermented syrups were made by boiling down the freshly
pressed juice of grapes to a fraction of its original bulk.
It is in fact feasible that syrups of this kind were used in
the very early days to sweeten wine after its fermentation.

The citizens of Jerez played no small part in the pre-
*Jerez and Columbus* parations for those enterprises of Christopher Columbus

40

which culminated in his discovery of America in 1492. Fray Jorge de Santiago, head of the Conventento de la Merced in Jerez organized aid for him; and in 1493 the citizens as a whole contributed 804 *fanegas* of wheat towards the stores for his second journey.

As to the town itself, G. W. Suter, Vice-Consul in *The town of Jerez* Jerez from 1831–87, described it as a large and disorganized place, where, after dark, it was advisable if not essential, to be accompanied by a servant with a torch in one hand and a cudgel in the other. Today however Jerez-de-la-Frontera is a clean well-lit township of some 100,000 inhabitants. And while it offers little of either architectural or artistic interest, save perhaps the venerable Moorish Castle, the Alcazar, the turrets and walls *The Alcazar* of which date from the eleventh century, and some fifteenth-century churches, it is a Mecca of wine lovers from the Globe over. For them the *Bodegas*, those vast *Bodegas* temples of wine, where Sherry is nursed, trained and matured for the delectation of the whole world, are the points of main interest.

Sandeman's Bodegas (overground wine stores) which are light, capacious and well ventilated, are approached through attractive gardens and forecourts; but these are the final resting places of the wines while they are still in Jerez. Let us therefore turn at once to the vineyards where Sherry has its birth.

THE SHERRY VINEYARDS

Visitors arriving at Jerez by either road or rail, frequently remark upon the apparent absence of vineyards, and express wonder as to where the grapes are grown. The answer is, that either mere chance or nature in beneficent mood decreed, that the best vineyard land should be situated away from both smoky railways and dusty high-roads.

Unlike the precipitous Port wine vineyards discussed heretofore, the terrain around Jerez-de-la-Frontera (100 to 500 feet above sea-level), where Sherry vines are reared, is gently undulating. This land is graded into three main groups or qualities from a viticultural point of view. First

*Albariza*

we have what is known as *albariza* soil which is compounded of 80% chalk with magnesia and clay. The

*Barro and arenas*

second is known as *barro, i.e.* clay; and the third group is *arenas* or sandy soil.

*Albariza* which produces the finest Sherries is found some five miles north and north-west of Jerez, in the Carrascal and Macharnudo districts; and it is here that

*Sandeman vineyards*

the Sandeman vineyards, 'El Corregidor' and 'Cerro Viejo' are situated. In these vineyards the vines are planted in rows five feet apart, to form squares which gives a coverage of some 2000 vines to the acre.

*Productivity*

On *albariza* soil this number of vines will produce an average of 7500 lb. of grapes, which will in turn make 500 gallons of Sherry. The crop from *barro* and *arenas* soil is somewhat higher, but its quality is not so fine.

*Cultivation of vines*

The vines are cultivated on a low trunk about 16 in. high, only four branches of which, supported by forked props where necessary (to keep the fruit off the ground), are allowed to grow. Of these four branches two in turn are permitted to produce fruit in alternate years.

The fruit is, by the way, so delicious that it is necessary to protect it, to which end elevated structures are built

*Bien-te-veo*

in the vineyards which are called *Bien-te-veo*. Literally translated *Bien-te-veo* means, I can see you alright, and from these towers armed guards keep watch to prevent theft of the grapes which are excellent eating.

Spain did not escape the dread scourge of *Phylloxera* *Vastatrix*, which was first observed in the Jerez vineyards in July 1894. Here, as in other wine-growing districts which were affected, the remedy was found by grafting the variety of native vine required, on American stock, the roots of which are immune from attack by these insects. While this had the effect of shortening the productive life of the native vines from some seventy to twenty-five years, it had no ill effect on the quality of the fruit. There is moreover an element of counterbalance in that the grafted vines bear fruit at an earlier age than did the original Spanish vines.

*Phylloxera*

A new grafted vineyard produces grapes in the fourth year, and the fruit of the fifth year is suitable for making wine; whereas the original vines did not produce wine until somewhat later. When their productiveness wanes, the vines are uprooted and the land is left fallow for some years to recuperate before new vines are planted.

The most common varieties of grape which are grown are *Palomino*, *Mantúo Castellano* and *Pedro Ximénez*. It is said that Pedro Ximénez grapes were brought from the Rhine by Pieter Siemens, a German soldier in Charles V's army and that his name, which was given to this fine fruit, became Pedro Ximénez in Spanish.

*Pieter Siemens*

We cannot leave our discussion of the vineyards without impressing upon the reader the axiom that *it is from the nature of the soil in the Jerez vineyards that this wine of infinite variety absorbs its distinctive and exclusive characteristics*. Sherry ranges from the very light and very driest of wine through a diversity of styles, to wines that are dark, rich and

*Importance of geological conditions*

sweet; one or other of which will have the approbation of the most fastidious palate. And it is only of Spanish Sherry that this can be said without fear of contradiction.

Unlike Port wine which, as we have seen, is protected in respect of its geographical and geological origin, Sherry does not as yet enjoy such a safeguard. It is nevertheless quite beyond dispute that *true Sherry*, which is without equal, *can come only from that area in Spain where the requisite geological conditions pertain.* To put a fine point on this fact – if a Jerez vine were transplanted in another part of the world it would not grow Sherry. Now let us turn to the Sherry vintage and some simple details of the method of making this wine.

### THE SHERRY VINTAGE

Nearly all the Sandeman vineyards are on *Albariza* soil, in the celebrated tracts of vineland known as Carrascal and Macharnudo, the pedigrees of which can be traced back for centuries. It is wines from these choice districts that have made Sandeman Sherries famous. Here, about *Vintage time* the second week in September, when the grapes are usually ripe, the vintagers go to work with their knives, lopping off bunches of luscious fruit which are placed in baskets and carried by mules to the vineyard house where the grapes are laid out in the sun on esparto-grass mats to dry and concentrate the juice.

The Pedro Ximénez grapes are cut first and pressed last. This gives them a fortnight in the sun, during which they become almost raisins regarding which we shall have more to say later.

The Palomino grapes on the other hand remain in the sun for twenty-four hours only.

The Alcazar, a venerable Moorish castle.

Vintagers at work on El Corregidor.

Grapes being sunned.

After this sunning, about 1500 lb. of grapes are placed in each *lagar*. These *lagars*, which stand on either timber trestles or stone pillars, are wooden troughs approximately 18 ft. square and 2 ft. deep in the centre of which is a pressing device known as the 'screw'.

*The lagars*

*The 'screw'*

The *lagars* being filled, two men, each wearing spiked rawhide boots, tramp up and down in them, breaking the skins of the grapes to express the first flow of juice. Then, after this initial treading, the crushed grapes are piled round the 'screw' and secured in position with a plaited grass strap. This accomplished, four men bind their wrists to the levers of the 'screw' with their sashes, and extract most of the remaining juice which runs into wooden tubs out of which it is ladled into butts holding approximately 108 gallons of wine.

Each pressing of 1500 lb. of grapes produces enough 'must' to fill seven-eighths of a butt, thus leaving room for the effects of fermentation and avoiding excessive loss due to bubbling over.

The butts of fermenting wine are then transported immediately to the *bodegas* in lorries, where they are laid out in the open during the first tumultuous fermentation, the odour of which pervades the city and environs at this time, when thousands of butts of fermenting 'must' are laid out in the district.

*Fast fermentation*

A slow fermentation succeeds which continues for some ten weeks, during which every vestage of sugar in the wine is converted into alcohol. This means of course that the resulting wine is absolutely dry (without sweetness). How then, you may ask, are sweet Sherries produced?

*Slow fermentation*

This is where *Pedro Ximénez* or P.X. as it is called in the trade, plays an important part. The reader will recollect

*Pedro Ximénez*

that the specially selected grapes set apart for the production of this wine (which is pressed exactly as described above) have been sunned until they are almost raisins. This ensures a high concentration of sugar in the fruit, which when pressed produces a thick sweet syrup; the fermentation of which is checked by being placed with a quantity of brandy whereby much of the sweetness is retained. The finished wine has a Baumé (sweetness measure) of 23 to 24 degrees. Thus we have an ideal medium for sweetening other Sherries as desired.

To sweeten the less expensive blends and wines of lighter and medium character, where Pedro Ximénez would tend to mask the distinctive qualities of the wine, Dulce which has a sweetness factor of about 8 degrees Baumé is used.

Dulce wine is made by running the 'must' into casks containing sufficient wine brandy to arrest the fermentation, which retains the desired sweetness. Unlike the grapes used for P.X. those used in the production of Dulce are not sunned. We turn now to the next phase in the production of this fascinating wine.

THE ANADAS

On completion of the second fermentation, the new wine is examined by experts cask by cask, and is either approved and marked for further consideration, or rejected.

The team of experts responsible for this important task is composed of the Bodega Manager (head taster in charge of the entire store of wines), his assistant and the *Capataz* or Bodega Foreman, who puts the Manager's instructions concerning the movement and treatment of the wines into effect.

During these inspections the *Capataz* carries several *Capataz*
glasses and a *Venencia*, which is used for taking samples
from the butts under inspection. A *Venencia* is a deep *Venencia*
narrow silver cup attached to one end of a flexible whale-
bone handle. With this device experts dip out a quantity
of wine through the bung-hole of the cask, then holding
the handle of the *Venencia* at about its centre, they raise
the silver cup aloft and cascade the wine from it into a
glass held in the other hand, without spilling a drop.
Should you visit Jerez you are advised not to attempt this
feat, if you respect either good wine or your clothes. It
takes long practice to acquire the art of using this simple
device correctly.

The approved wine is then drawn off its lees, *i.e.* the
deposit which has fallen to the bottom of the cask, and is
put into fresh casks to develop in the *Anada*. This word *Anada*
*Anada* derives from the Latin *anno*, year, and signifies a
number of casks containing the wine of a particular year,
or what might be called a vintage wine. This is however
the only occasion on which Sherry is seen as a vintage
wine.

With the notable exception of the P.X. and Dulce wine,
we are still dealing here with completely dry (sugarless)
wine of no particular type; for it is not possible to
determine its type until three or four years after the
vintage.

Strange though it may seem, the contents of each cask
may differ from the others, even though the wine in each
was pressed at the same time under identical conditions.
The wide selection of types which emanate from a single
vineyard, is one of the mysteries and charms of Sherry.
And it should be remembered, these differences of type

result from natural causes without man's interference.

At the end of their sojourn in the *Anada* a sample is taken from each cask in turn and examined by sight and nose (smell) only; after which each cask is marked according to the type of its contents. In this way several main types of Sherry emerge. We have the *Finos* which are the lightest in both body and colour of all Sherries. These light straw-coloured wines of very fine bouquet are always retained as dry wines. Then there are the *Amontillados* which, while like the *Finos* in their basic stage, are fuller bodied and gain in both body and colour, meanwhile acquiring a pleasantly round bouquet. The *Amontillados* are usually blended into medium-dry wines.

The fragrant full-bodied *Olorosos* which attain a fine golden colour with age, are always blended into rich wines. And the *Rayas* which are not so fine as the *Olorosos*, but have good body and become deep amber as they mature, are an ideal base for many Brown Sherries.

There are, of course, many gradations of style between these types, but it is usually possible to allocate all wines to one or other of the main types. At this point the wines are transferred once again to fresh casks, grouped into types and kept in reserve for the next stage of their development. Until now the wine has been allowed to develop its own characteristics; but hereafter it will come under the control of the bodega manager, who will nurse and train it to follow its calling in the *Criaderas* and *Soleras*, towards which we now move *via* our discussion of the system employed to mature Sherry.

*The casks are marked*

*Finos*

*Amontillados*

*Olorosos*

*Rayas*

*Criaderas*

## SOLERAS

*The Solera system*   What is known as the *Solera* system of maturing wines is the method whereby Sherries are developed and matured, each within its own type, to the style and quality which is required to assure uniformity in the final blends. In this system wines of identical types are kept in groups of casks in ascending grades of maturity and age. The earlier grades are called *Criaderas*, and wines in the final stage of maturity are called *Soleras*. The method of operating the system calls for both care and experience of a high order.

The blender draws the amount of wine necessary for his blend from the *Solera*. He then replaces what he has taken from the *Solera* with the same amount of wine from the first (oldest and most mature) *Criadera*. This in turn is replenished from the second *Criadera* and so on through all the grades, a quantity of younger and less mature wine moving forward progressively. There may be as many as twelve stages in this process.

The enormous advantage of the *Solera* system is, that it ensures continuous supplies of wine of exactly the same style and age, for use in producing blends which can on this account be repeated indefinitely and with exactitude. This unerring continuity of style is assured, because as small quantities of the younger and less mature wines are moved up cask by cask towards the *Solera*, each takes on the precise character and nature of the wine into which it is placed, and becomes identical with it. This is nature's handiwork.

It is a matter of considerable importance that, after fermentation, Sherry derives much of its exclusive character from a yeast known as *flor del vino* (flower of wine), which grows naturally on the wine. This flower develops profusely on *Fino*, but somewhat less actively on *Oloroso* and *Raya*. The 'flower of wine' consumes oxygen

*'Flower of wine'*

avidly, and on this account the casks are left open to the air. They are, moreover, only seven-eighths filled to leave room in the casks for the development of the 'flower'. This facilitates examination of the wine and is the direct cause of some 5% evaporation *per annum*, which accelerates the process of maturing considerably by concentrating the bouquet.

Twice a year in Spring and Autumn, after its periods of activity, the 'flower of wine' falls to the bottom of the *Mother of the Wine* cask where it forms a crust known as 'Mother of the Wine' which has a marked influence on both the style and character of the Sherry. Great care is therefore taken not to break this beneficial deposit.

BLENDING

As marketed, all Sherries are to a greater or lesser extent blended wines. It is consequently to the blender's skill, and knowledge of the wines at his disposal, that we owe the wide range of Sherries one or other of which cannot fail to please every taste and prove ideal for any occasion.

The number of wines in a blend is not limited, but it must be appreciated that blending Sherry is not merely a matter of mixing wines together. Long experience and an intimate knowledge of those wines which will combine to form a homogeneous whole is essential, if the final result is to be in all respects a single wine. This perfect union of *Marrying wine* various wines, which is known as 'marrying', may take months to accomplish, the actual time needed varying with the wines which it is desired to blend.

It is perhaps appropriate here to mention that unlike *Sherry darkens* Port wine, which loses colour with age, Sherry acquires *with age* colour with the passage of time. It may therefore happen that the wine which you purchase as a very pale Sherry may gain some colour before you use it. This is however a natural process which does not change its essential character as a beverage. In this connection we take the opportunity to say that all Sandeman Sherries are freshly bottled in brilliant condition ready for immediate consumption; and they will if properly treated, remain bright in bottle for months. If however some Sherries are kept in bottle longer than six months (approximately) they will probably become cloudy and throw a sediment. This is a perfectly natural development, and it is one of the mysteries of nature that they are most prone to throw a sediment when the sap is either rising or falling in the vine than at any other time of the year.

Should your Sherry not be quite clear, stand the bottle *Decanting* upright for a short while before use, then pour it carefully into a decanter, leaving the sediment at the bottom of the bottle. The richer and fuller-bodied wines are the most suitable Sherries for keeping in bottle. It is however, generally speaking, preferable to purchase Sherry for ready use. It cannot be too strongly emphasized that wines are alive and their life continues in bottle in contra- *Wine is alive* distinction to distilled spirits, hence the phenomenon to which we refer.

MISCELLANEA

What we have said regarding the cellarage of and the glasses and decanters for use with Port wine, is equally applicable to Sherry and need not therefore be repeated.

YOUR SHERRY PARTY

Having thus summarily dismissed the keeping of and

receptacles for serving Sherry, let us turn to those cheerful and increasingly popular foregatherings which have come to be known as Sherry parties.

Armed with some dry, medium and rich Sherry, you are in a position to meet your friends' every taste. Add to this some of those little delicacies which make a universal appeal at these most pleasant functions and the success of your party is assured. Among these mouth-watering items there may be sandwiches containing either shrimp, *foie gras*, smoked salmon, assorted cheese, lobster, etc., etc.

One may serve also *Croutes* of crab, ham, chicken, tongue, smoked trout and even the humble but tasty kipper. And why not such sundries as assorted nuts either salted, plain or devilled, chipolatas, and cheese straws? With a selection from these, a liberal supply of skewer sticks, and plenty of ash-trays, there will be scant likelihood of complaint from any quarter.

### SHERRY AND COOKING

Wine is sadly neglected as a cooking medium in this country. And where Sherry is concerned, the entirely erroneous idea is prevalent that inferior wine 'is good enough' for use as an embellishment for foods and sauces. So much is this so, that the phrase 'Cooking Sherry', which indicates lack of quality, is commonplace. We will allow ourselves the masterly understatement that any such idea is grossly misguided. On the contrary, wines selected for use in the preparation and improvement of foods must harmonize with the other ingredients with which it is used, if a really pleasing final result is to be achieved. Thus it may be desirable to use either a dry, medium or sweet Sherry, and this should always be of that quality

The 'screw', a device for pressing wine after the initial treading.

Tumultuous fermentation.

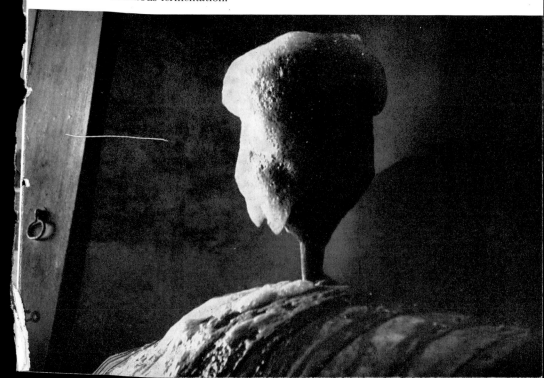

A landing of Sandeman Sherry in the London docks.

which will enhance the flavour of the dish. Wine is not used in cooking merely to add alcohol; and if a wine is not worthy of its place in a glass, it has no place in cuisine.

Having made this important point, it is our pleasure to advance some culinary suggestions and recipes for the use of Sherry. Who will not admit that it is often the sauce which makes a dish?

As a base for other sauces Brown Sauce is both excellent *Brown Sauce* and commendably economical. First bake some flour in a hot oven until it becomes light brown in colour. Now mix it into a paste with butter and add either veal or shin-beef stock, onions, thyme and bay leaves to taste; cook it for two hours, add a liberal quantity of Sandeman 'Three Star Brown' Sherry, and pass it through a fine tammy.

Put a large glass of either Sandeman 'Three Star Brown' *Sauce Financiére* or 'Brown Bang' Sherry into a stewpan with essence of truffles and a little cayenne pepper and reduce it to half. Then add a ladleful of Brown Sauce (as above) and boil it for five minutes, after which pass the sauce through a tammy into a bain-marie for use with sweetbreads, veal, etc.

Place the trimmings of the birds selected for your Salmi *Salmi Sauce* into a stew-pan with a little olive oil, four shallots, one bay leaf and a sprig of thyme, and heat them for five minutes. Next, add two glasses of Sandeman 'Three Star Brown' or 'Brown Bang' Sherry and reduce to half. Then add a ladleful of Brown Sauce and some mushroom essence to taste, set it to boil and leave it near the fire to clarify. After being skimmed and passed through a tammy into a bain-marie it is ready to serve with any salmi, *i.e.* duck, chicken, partridge, pheasant, etc.

That the suitable addition of Sherry to many foods

will enhance them beyond belief can be put to the test quite easily.

*A simple experiment*  For example, the addition of a glass of Sandeman 'Three Star Brown' Sherry to a thick cream sauce, for use with chicken, turns this often commonplace dish into a gourmet's joy.

And there are many soups, especially consommé (either hot or cold), which are greatly improved by the addition of either dry or rich Sherry according to taste.

A liberal addition of 'Three Star Brown' or 'Brown Bang' Sherry when cooking a ham, impregnates the flesh with the flavour of the wine to an extent which renders the ham an epicure's delight.

Oysters are not everyone's delicacies, but for those who enjoy these piquant bi-valves, the accompaniment of a glass of dry Sherry will add to their zest. You will, we think, find also that a glass of rich 'Brown Bang' Sherry with a slice of really fruity cake taken at mid-morning will tend to brighten the rest of the day.

Yes, there are innumerable occasions and circumstances when one or other of the wide range of Sandeman Sherries will add considerably to your gastronomic pleasure. Your morning grapefruit will taste as good again if you prepare it the night before, sprinkle a little sugar on it then add a dash of dry Sherry; Sandeman 'Apitiv' is ideal.

Many fruits, plums, pears and fruit salads generally, are much improved by the addition of a little Sandeman Sherry. Why restrict its use to the ubiquitous trifle? A little thought and experiment will extend our few suggestions vastly, but space forbids our extension of them here.

Here then at the end of our discourse on two of the